BIGFOOT

A NEW REALITY

By Melissa George

Cover Illustration Copyright © 2020 by Melissa George

Cover design by Melissa George

Book design and production by Melissa George

Cover Images from Morgue File, or personal images.

Research for Authenticity, Cari George, Marty George, Chris George

Names and places have been changed to protect people and properties.

This story has been vetted for truth and authenticity.

Before you begin, please let me remind you that I am an Independent Author. I create my books. They are all written in General Casual. If you find the occasional Typo. I apologize. I don't have a group of people sitting in their office waiting to go over my book before it reaches you. The English used in the majority of my books may not be proper at times. This is better to convey the story to you just as it was told to me without sounding like a textbook. With this being said, I hope you enjoy this book cover to cover. If you do, please think about leaving me a review. Your reviews can make or break an independent author. If you didn't care for the book. I understand. We can't connect with every book. Just try to go easy on me with your review. Thank you.

This is not a work of fiction. However some names and places in the book have been changed to keep the identity of the people involved private.

Contents

Chapter 1

My wife and I were currently looking for a new house. We had lived in the suburbs the whole time the kids were growing up. It was easier that way. The kids were closer to school and friends. And I didn't have far to drive to get to work. Our youngest one, now twenty-six, had finally moved out. I had recently retired, and my wife worked from home. So we were looking for something smaller and a bit more private. I wanted something out in the woods, preferably where I could hunt and fish. Jen wanted a vegetable and flower garden. We enjoyed being outdoors, but living in town limited that. I had grown up in the Appalachian mountains, and that is where I hoped to find a place now. The woods and the rivers were calling to me. I just couldn't wait to catch some of those fresh mountain trout.

One evening I was looking through the real estate ads, and I found a place that looked promising. The add said rustic, two bedrooms, two bath cabin with loft. Open Kitchen and dining area, stone-hued fireplace. Two car garage with washroom. Large back deck overlooking Pignut Mountain. Cabin with sixty-three acres. I was already sold. I was ready to move tomorrow! But, I knew Jen would want to see the place first. Now let me add that Pignut Mountain lies within Shenandoah National Park, well the summit of it does. So that put part of the Shenandoah River on the property. I was in heaven.

I could just imagine my days of fishing. Being that the property
butted up against the national forest, the whitetail deer had to be
plentiful too.

I showed the add with the few pictures to Jen. I was hoping that
she would like it as much as I did. We made plans with the real
estate agent to meet up and tour the property. It would be an
easy three-hour drive each way. But we could make it a day trip
and still be back home that evening. I set it up to be out there
two days from now, and that still wasn't quick enough for me.

The drive out was pleasant and uneventful. We had beautiful
spring weather with a crisp blue sky. The kind of weather that
lets you know that the heat of Summer is just around the corner.

The agent, Steven, was waiting for us at the driveway to the
cabin. We pulled in behind his Rover. My first impression was
that this looked more like an old logging road than a driveway.
As if he had read my mind, Steven walked over to our truck.

"I'm glad to see you are driving a four-wheel drive," he said, with
his hand extended. He stood about six feet tall with salt and
pepper hair.
He gave a big smile that exposed perfect teeth. "That driveway
hasn't been used in a long time, and it may get rough," he said,
motioning toward the narrow dirt road. I shook hands with him
and laughed. "Well, we told you we wanted rural," I said.

He extended his hand to Jen as she walked around the front of the truck. "Is this the actual driveway"? She asked hesitantly.

"I don't think it's as bad as it looks," Steven said. "But one of the benefits of this cabin is that it's very rural. You will have all the privacy you could want. As a matter of fact, that is why the last family moved into town. It was just too secluded for the wife".

"Let's go take a look," I said eagerly. I was anxious to see if this would be our new home. And I didn't need Steven saying anything that could influence Jen not to want to move.

After just a short way down the drive, I realized why Steven had mentioned the four-wheel drive. The driveway was a narrow dirt road that was almost taken over by the surrounding woods. Branches brushed against the car as we drove, making horrible screeching sounds. The driveway itself was rough and bumpy. It even appeared to be washed out in some areas.

It was a rough ride, to say the least. I assumed it was too far out to be zoned for county maintenance. When you move out to the country, you have to deal with things like this on your own.

I glanced over at Jen, she had both hands on the dashboard and was bouncing up and down in her seat. At times when it got rough. I would hear her suck in her breath. I wondered if this would change her mind about the property.

"You know I can have this scraped," I said.

"Why?" she said with a laugh. "It sure will cut down on unwanted salesmen."

We both laughed out loud as we bounced along the dirt drive. My Jen was a real trooper. Always up for an adventure. That's one thing I loved about her.

I was beginning to wonder if this was actually a driveway or just a backwoods road when it finally gave way to a clearing. The cabin sat on a circular drive. Steve rolled down a slight hill to the garage. I stopped where we were. My first impression was, "There has to be a mistake in the paperwork. There is no way we could ever afford this place." From where we sat, I was looking at a beautiful cabin with a large front porch. Granite walk stones made a path to the front door.

 To the left of the house was the small garage that I assumed led into the kitchen. The yards were once well-manicured; this looked like it should be in a brochure. It was closely surrounded by thick woods, and you could see the Pignut Mountain over the top of the house.

"Oh my," Jen said. "I wasn't expecting this at all."
I could tell that just like me, she was pleasantly surprised.

We both got out of the vehicle as Steven walked up to meet us.

"Are you guys ready for the grand tour"? He asked.
I didn't say so, but I was ready to find the river!

Steven led us down the stone path and into the front door.
Entering the living room, I was instantly surrounded by Western
Red Cedar. Even the beams in the high ceiling sported this
beautiful wood.

The living room, dining room, and kitchen were all open space. It
was smaller than what we had been used to. But it was precisely
what we were looking for. Straight up, above the living room was
the loft. I knew right away; that was where Jen would be
working. She was a freelance columnist and made pretty good
money at it. (This is also why I have had Melissa change our
names in this book.) I looked over at Jen, and I could already see
her arranging furniture in her mind. I was excited to see that she
liked the place.
We checked out the bed and bathrooms. They were your average
rooms, nothing special, plenty big enough for us. And there was
enough space when the kids came to visit.

Coming back into the living room, Steven walked over and
opened the floor-length drapes. Jen and I both gasped! The view
was unlike anything I had ever seen before! There was a set of
french doors that opened onto the porch. Steven unlocked these
and opened them both. The fresh mountain air quickly engulfed
the room.

The panoramic view was breathtaking! The whole east wall of the living room was large floor-length windows with beautiful French doors set in the center. I was even surer now that there had to be a mistake on the price.

We all walked out onto the back deck. There was a Jacuzzi to the far left and a swing to the right. But the view was what had us mesmerized.

The deck was about seven feet off the ground because the back yard sloped down where it stopped at the foot of the Shenandoah River! I could see the river from the porch! I wanted to grab Steven and hug him, but I figured that wouldn't be such a good idea.

Jen looked at me with a big smile on her face. Well, all three of us were grinning from ear to ear.
Jen and I knew this was our new home, and Steven knew he had just made a sale. I would spend the rest of my life paying for this place if I had to.

As we left the house, Steven took us out through the kitchen door so that we could see the garage and the washroom. The washroom was just off of the garage with a back door leading to the outside. On the other side of the door was a small plateau that held a clothesline and an excellent area for Jen's little garden. This house was unbelievably perfect for us.

The garage was large enough for me to turn into my work area. Now I wouldn't have to worry about nosy neighbors hanging out in my garage to see what I was building. If I wanted to make a chest of drawers or an end table, there wouldn't be someone standing around telling me I should have done it differently or hoping I would give it to them when I finished.

We walked out into the back yard. It was rather large and private. There was a fire pit with a picnic table down near the river, and a small storage shed that set back in the woods just past the garage. The shed matched the wood of the house perfectly, making it almost invisible.

"Are you up for a hike"? Steven asked.

"A hike,"? Jen replied quickly.
I had no clue what he was talking about; he must have seen my confusion because he laughed and responded, " Sixty-three acres come with this property."

"Oh My"! Jen exclaimed. "Do we have to walk that today"? I could tell by the look on her face that she was about to beat a hasty retreat to the comfort of the truck while Steven and I drug ourselves through sixty-three acres of dense woods.

"No, you don't have to," He replied. "The boundaries are marked with stakes and orange flags. It's just an offer; I can show you the land, or you can explore it at your leisure later on.

Jen looked at me, and her eyes were saying, "There is no way in hell I am walking all over these woods. Get us out of this."

"Thanks, Steve," I replied, giving my warmest smile. "I would love to go down and look at the river, but unfortunately, we have a long drive home. So I guess we need to wrap this up.

"I completely understand," He responded, looking a bit relieved himself. "Have you two made a decision yet"?

Jen 's eye met mine with a smile.

"Yep." I replied, "we'll be taking the house.' I felt my heart skip a beat, just hearing myself say this.
After locking up the house, we all walked outside, where Steven ducked into his car for his briefcase. He tossed it up on the hood and opened it. He sorted through some paperwork before bringing out a few for us to sign.

Jen and I both signed his papers and shook his hand. I took a quick look at the numbers again and couldn't believe how cheap this place was priced. There had to be a reason. I scolded myself for thinking this way. It was nothing more than a secluded cabin that had been reduced to sell. After the papers were signed, Steve handed over the keys, telling us we could move in whenever we liked.

I looked at the cabin one last time before we left. I felt like a kid at Christmas. I had just bought the house I had always wanted at an amazingly low price. After selling the home in town, I would have enough left over to add a work shed if we chose to.

Driving down the bumpy driveway, Jen reaches over and lays her hand on my leg. "I love our cabin," she said with a smile.

At that moment, all was right with the world.

Chapter 2

It took us a couple of weeks to get everything together and moved up to the cabin. Jen and our two daughters had held a couple of yard sales for the things we wouldn't be bringing. The things that remained were either given out among the kids or shipped off to the thrift store. We had minimized our belongings and were looking forward to a new life full of peace, quiet, and calm.

Our first full day in our new house was beautiful. We were acting like teenagers again, Laughing and teasing each other as we worked to put things away. I can tell you it felt different, not having three teenagers and their friends in my kitchen. As we put food in the cabinets, Jen dropped a fresh quart of Apple butter. It hit right between the rug and the tile. Apple butter flew across the room, leaving a sticky mess in its wake. I took the small, oval rug outside and hosed it off. I then lay it across the rail on the back porch to air dry. I looked out over the mountains. I still couldn't believe I was home. I planned to do a little fishing tomorrow and maybe check out the woods for signs of deer.

Jen and I were sitting in the living room watching TV before bed. She had gone into the kitchen to grab us a snack when I heard her yell, "Hey Matt, can you grab the rug for me"?

I had forgotten all about putting the rug out on the rail earlier. I walked out on the porch and walked straight to the mat. It wasn't there. I looked down on the porch to see if it had fallen. It wasn't there either. I went back to the door and turned the lights on. I leaned out over the rail and looked down into the yard. It wasn't down there. How did a rug just disappear? Maybe Jen had thrown it into the washer and forgot.

I went to the kitchen where she was. "The rug isn't on the deck." "Did you throw it in the wash"? I asked.

"No," she said, turning to look at me. "You took it out while I cleaned up."

"Well, it isn't there now," I called over my shoulder, heading back to the living room. " I'll go out and look for it tomorrow." That was the last time either of us thought of the rug for a while.

The next morning Jen and I opened the curtains so we could watch the sunrise over the mountain. I could not believe how beautiful it was. There were a few clouds that caught the glare of the sun, turning them from white to gold, yellow, and orange.

I tried to talk Jen into hiking with me, but she claimed she still had some things to get done in the house. I knew when I got back; I would find her curled up on the swing with her nose buried in a book. But that was perfectly fine with me. We had both put in a few days of hard work getting the house set up.

I grabbed my backpack with a couple of bottles of water, my compass, a pack of crackers, a notebook, and a pencil. I would be scoping out hunting and fishing areas. Then hopefully, tomorrow, I could get back out there for some well-awaited fishing.

I kissed Jen on the cheek and told her it would be late afternoon before I got back. Walking out the door, it occurred to me that we didn't get a cell phone signal out here. I would have to pick us up a couple of handheld radios.

I headed down across the back yard toward the river. The river was about twenty feet across and pretty calm at this point. I thought if I walked the rocks carefully, I should be able to make it across without a problem. I knew Jen would be up in the house watching me. I didn't want to wind up sitting in the middle of the cold water for her entertainment.

I made it across without incident. I turned to the house and waved. Jen waved from the back deck. I knew she would be watching. I chuckled to myself and headed deeper into the woods.

It didn't take long to find a game trail to follow. Without it, the hike would have been slow going. The woods looked like they had never been traversed by human feet. The underbrush was thick from years of growing wild; this would be perfect for deer hunting. I walked, enjoying the smell of the woods and the birds chirping overhead.

I found a couple of areas where the deer had been bedding and what looked to be some wild hog ruts. Being happy with my find, I decided to turn my thoughts on fishing now. I had just turned around to start back down the trail when I heard a deep grunt. It sounded like a cross between a deer and a bear. I stood silently and listened for a jaw pop that would let me know if the sound had come from a distressed bear. I didn't hear anything follow the grunt. The woods had gone silent. By silent, I mean eerily quiet. The birds had stopped chirping. And there were no squirrels in sight; this in itself was odd as the squirrels had flanked me since I had entered the woods.

I had done a good bit of hunting and fishing with my dad and grandfather when I was younger, but I couldn't remember the woods ever being this silent. The tiny hairs on the back of my neck stood up, and I had the distinct feeling of being watched. I wished now I had brought my gun with me. It was a stupid move to leave home without it. Looking back on it, I couldn't remember a time I had ever been in the woods without A gun.

Being anxious had caused me to make a bad mistake. It was time to head back now. I didn't want to come face to face with a bear. I started back down the game trail the way I had come up; this was the first time I realized just how wide this trail was. Most game trails are only a couple of feet wide. But this one was about four feet wide: This struck me as odd. You don't usually find a game trail this broad.

It was early afternoon when I crossed the river again. I stood on the rocks for a minute to see if there were trout in the water. To my amazement, this river was just full of them. Every thirty seconds, one or two would swim by the rock I was on. As I stood there watching them, I heard the grunt again. It didn't sound as close to me this time. But I knew I would get my gun when I got my fishing gear.

I sat there on the edge of the river fishing with my rifle propped up next to me. I had talked Jen into coming down and sitting by the water.

To start with, she had been reluctant to come down to the river after she saw me get my gun. I explained to her that it was just a precaution until we knew more about the wildlife in the area. I wasn't about to tell her what had happened today.

Jen had grown up on the outskirts of Atlanta, Georgia. She was born a city girl. Since we were married, she had gone on the family camping trips and would fish with me from time to time. But she would let you know rather quickly that she had no desire to go hunting. Just the thought of bears and mountain lions would send her straight into the house. I had tried on many occasions to explain to her that a chance encounter with one of these animals was rather slim. But I think her mind held an image of upon entering the woods; they would immediately hunt you down, knock you over and commence to eating you on the spot.

I knew if I had told her what happened today, we would both be in the house now, probably with all the doors and windows closed up.

The fish were biting good, and I was completely relaxed. It had been many years since I had felt such inner peace. Growing up in the Appalachian mountains had taught me to enjoy nature. Nothing compared to being out in the woods far away from cell phones and computers. It was a simpler way of life that many people had lost touch with.

"Did you hear that"? Jen's voice plunged me back to reality. She had put her book down and was looking over her shoulder toward the woods.

"What did you hear"? I asked. Now remembering the grunts, I had heard earlier.

" I'm not sure," she said softly. "It was sort of a grunt, but kind of like a growl." She looked at me concerned and then back toward the woods.

I didn't hear anything, but I thought it might not be a bad idea for me to take her on up to the house. The sun was beginning to set, and with no one has lived here for a while, the wildlife might have grown comfortable coming in closer than they usually would.

I stood up and pulled my stringer of fish out of the water. "Why don't we go cook these for dinner," I said. Looking at the six beautiful trout on my stringer.

" I'm all for that," she responded. Giving the now darkening woods one last look over her shoulder.

I picked up my gun and handed her the stringer of fish. We walked up across the back yard as the sun turned the western sky a fiery red.

I cleaned the fish in the garage as Jen prepared the side dishes to go with our fresh catch. It wasn't long before we were both out on the back deck with the grill going.

Jen had set the stereo to a country station and left the french doors open so that we could hear it. I kept thinking just how lucky we were to have gotten this place so cheap. I was living my childhood dream by being here, and I believe Jen loved it every bit as much as I did.

The fish was the best I had eaten in many years. We lingered over the last of our coffee as we enjoyed the spring evening.

I got up and turned off the stereo as Jen took the dishes to the kitchen. I wanted to hear the night sounds: the frogs and the crickets. Just as I settled back into my chair, I heard a noise coming from the river. I sat there, straining my ears to see if it would happen again.
I could hear Jen moving around in the kitchen and considered calling her out here to see if she would hear it too, but she returned to her chair just as I was about to call her. I sat there quietly, waiting then it happened again.

"What in the world"... Her voice trailed off as she looked down at the river. It was pitch black down there. There was no way we could see anything. "What was that"? She asked, her eyes still glued to the dark terrain.

" I have no idea," I responded, as another rock landed in the river. You could tell that these were easily five-pound rocks by the splash they made, and then sometimes it would hit another rock with a loud thud.

" Is that rocks being thrown in the river"? She asked me.

I, too, thought that was what it sounded like, but there was just no plausible way that could be happening. There were no houses, even remotely close to us, so that ruled out the possibility of kids goofing off. (This was something I would not miss in moving away from the suburbs.)

"That is what it sounds like," I told her. "But it's just not possible. There are no other houses around here".

She thought for a moment and then said, "campers?"

Now I guess that could be possible. There could be someone camping on up the river. We listened as another rock hit the water. I stood up and walked over to the rail. "Stop that and get out of here"! I yelled. We heard what sounded like some rustling in the bushes, and then everything was quiet. Eerily quiet. There were no nighttime sounds at all.

'Maybe it was just some kids," Jen said, settling back into her chair.

I was wondering how hard it would be to get a night light set up on a large pole down by the water. I didn't like the yard being so dark. While I was at it, I could put some lights out front too.

" I'm going to take a shower," Jen said, standing up and going into the house.

Chapter 3

I walked down to the river the next morning after breakfast. I couldn't tell if there were any rocks out of place because of the water moving. If any had been thrown into the river, they looked like they belonged there now.

I looked around, trying to decide where the best place would be to put up my light. I stood in different spots facing the house, trying to get the best angle. That's when I noticed there had already been a hole dug. I knelt and moved the grass back; there were still some concrete remnants and some rotted wood down inside the hole. It appeared as if the last pole here had rotted away. It looked like a good place to me, and half of my work was already complete. A quick trip to the hardware store, and I would have some lights up before dark.

I asked Jen if she wanted to ride into town, but she declined. Our daughter was supposed to be bringing our two dogs up today, and Jen had missed them terribly. I was looking forward to them getting here myself. They were three-year-old Boxer Bulldogs, a brother and sister pair Brutus, and Bella. Brutus was high strung and into everything where Bella was more laid back.

I was glad Jen had mentioned them coming today. I would need to get some fencing at the store. I wanted to get the back yard fenced in for them. I could trust Bella to stay in the yard, but Brutus would be two counties over chasing rabbits if I didn't confine him. It looked like my day had just gotten busy. I might as well get started, I thought.

The local hardware was rather small but happened to have everything I needed, right down to the handheld radios I had wanted. Tom and Nancy Sullivan owned the store. They were a lovely couple, and we hit it off right away. When I told them that we had just moved to town, Nancy insisted that she would bake a cake and bring it by the house. I told them to come by anytime. Tom couldn't wait to do some fishing. I hopped into my truck, knowing that Jen would be thrilled that I had invited them over. Jen loved having a house full of people, and she was always the perfect hostess.

As I neared the house on our bumpy driveway, I was greeted By Brutus and Bella. They apparently recognized the sound of my truck and escaped up the road to great me. If Jen had seen them, there would have been hell to pay for leaving the yard. I leaned over and opened the passenger door. Both dogs scrambled to get into the vehicle with me. I laughed out loud as they attacked with a barrage of wet tongues and tail wags. I think I might have been as happy to see them as they were me. But we won't tell anyone that. I waited a minute for them to calm down and drove on down the driveway.

Gretchen's little Toyota was parked in the upper part of the drive in front of the house. I bet she had a heck of a time with these two big dogs in such a little car. I wondered why she hadn't driven Randy's suburban. I had just assumed she would with the dogs. Being that Brutus liked to help me drive, I always crated them in the back. I don't see how in the world she fought him off and drove the whole way here.

I let the dogs out, and they immediately ran to the kitchen door. It looked like they already knew their way around. I let them inside and began to unload the things from my truck into the backyard. I had every intention of getting the light up first but with the dogs being here now. I would be working on their fence.

Jen and Gretchen, flanked by the mutt team, came out on the deck to supervise. I threw my hand up to wave and began laying out the posts for the fence.

It was nearing sunset as I attached the gate to the fence. It had taken me all afternoon to fence in the backyard, but it was done now, and I was happy with it.

It was time to get the dogs and sample whatever it was that Jen and Gretchen were grilling. I had smelled it for the past hour, and it had my stomach growling.

I fastened my fence to the siding at the back door of the washroom. All we had to do was let the dogs out the kitchen door into the garage, through the washroom, and they were out. I knew that it would only be a couple of days, and they would be running this gauntlet like it was second nature.

"Wow," Gretchen brought steaks"? I asked, snagging a small piece from the platter near the grill. "I'm highly impressed," I said, teasing my daughter.

She punched me in the shoulder, saying, " I knew you would try to feed me bologna, so I brought us some real food."

"It's good to see you, baby," I said, kissing her on top of her head.

"Come on, you two"! I called to the dogs heading back through the kitchen. "It's time for you to check out your new yard." Just like planned, they followed me through the garage and into the washroom. I opened the back door and watched them rush out like wild bulls. The far corner of the yard was completely dark, but I knew there was no way these two could get out. I had dug the fence four feet into the ground, and it was five feet tall above ground. This should deter any digging or jumping that they may decide to do. I left them to their exploring and headed back in for more of that steak.

The steak dinner had been nice after working all afternoon. And now the three of us enjoyed a cup of coffee as we listened to the crickets and bullfrogs. The night air was a little chilly, but we were well into spring now, and Summer was coming fast.

Brutus's loud bark shattered my thoughts. It sounded like he was at the lower part of the yard near the river, and he was really going off the Richter scale. "Brutus Quiet"! I called out. This worked for all of five seconds. That command usually stopped his bark but not tonight. He saw or smelled something. I reluctantly got up to go get the flashlight. I would walk down and take a look. I was kicking myself for not getting the light up.

Just as I stepped out the washroom door into the backyard, the smell hit me. It was the worst smell I had ever experienced. It seemed to be a cross between rotting meat and wet dog. I immediately buried my face in my T-shirt and began yelling for the dogs.

Where in the world was this smell coming from? Did we have a sewer line around here anywhere? I hesitantly started to walk down across the yard, shining the light as I went. Brutus was still down in the lower yard barking, but Bella was now running full circles around me, thrilled that I had come out to play.

Luckily, as I neared Brutus, the smell had begun to fade. He was in the far corner of the yard, barking at something toward the river. I shined my light in that direction, panning it slowly up and down the bank. I had assumed a small animal might have come down to fish, and Brutus was giving him a warning that this part of the river was taken now. As I slowly moved the light, Bella had gotten brave. She threw her feet up on the fence and let out a couple of deep long yelps that any hunting dog would have been proud of.

"OK, you two, that's enough." I scolded. " Come on," I commanded, turning back toward the house. Like disappointed children, they fell into step with me, and the three of us headed inside.

'What was up with them"? Jen asked as I stepped back out onto the porch. She had poured me a fresh cup of coffee while I was out with the dogs. I picked up the cup and carried it over to my recliner. As I sat down, I put both of my feet up and sipped.

" I'm assuming Brutus was making enemies with the local wildlife. I never did see anything. But that had to be what set him off", I told her.

"What in the world was that horrible smell"? Gretchen asked. I had thought I was going to lose my steak before it went away".

'I'm not sure", I answered. " I will have to check the place out tomorrow for an exposed sewer pipe. I sure didn't want that fragrance wafting across the yard when we had people over to visit.

The three of us sat and chatted late into the evening. Having Gretchen with us was nice. She would be heading back in the morning, and I knew Jen would be moping around the house all day missing her. Maybe I could get her out in the yard with me as I put up the lights.

Chapter 4

I had to agree with Jen; it was sad to see Gretchen leave this morning. But she promised to come back for a week in the Summer to do some hiking and fishing. That gave us something to look forward to.

I had been digging the hole for the outside light as my mind drifted from Gretchen to the reason I was putting this light up. The strange growls I had heard. Maybe with the light on, the wildlife would start avoiding this area. I had no idea what had made the noise I had heard, but something told me it had to be a big animal. I already felt better with the yard being fenced in now. That would provide an excellent barrier for some of the wildlife.

It was late afternoon by the time I got the back yard light up and added some motion detector lights to all sides of the house. Jen had come out a few times to try to get me to take a break. I just wanted to be finished with the project and not have to worry about it later.

Now that I had finished working, I walked up to the house to let Bella and Brutus out. I had made them stay inside most of the day because I didn't want to have to chase down my tools as I tried to work.

I loved those two beasts, but they sure could be a nuisance. As if reading my mind Jen released them, and they both came across the yard at me like two military tanks. I began to laugh well before they knocked me off my feet.

After my shower, I went into the kitchen, hoping for a cup of coffee. As I passed the French doors, I saw Jen and the dogs standing out on the deck. Jen was looking out at the mountain, and all of Brutus's hair was standing on end. I opened the door to step out, and both dogs nearly knocked me over! Bella ran into our bedroom while Brutus jumped up on the couch.

"What in the world," I said as I walked out the door.

"Shhhhh"!!! Replied Jen.
She pointed at the mountain and whispered at the same time. "Something over there is screaming."

I stood there beside her and silently waited. After a couple of minutes, I heard a scream as I had never heard before. It was eerie yet fascinating. I stood there, hoping to hear it again. It wasn't long before the odd scream came again.

"What is that"? Jen whispered.

"I have no idea," I told her. "I don't think I have ever heard that before."

We heard the scream a few more times, but we could tell it was moving up the mountain. Once the screaming stopped, there were no other sounds. No frogs or crickets, just the sound of the river down below us. I thought it was odd for the night to be so still. I didn't think to mention it to Jen as we went in to watch TV.

Both dogs joined us in the living room, and the events of the evening were all forgotten as we watched people trying to survive on some Island.

The next evening I went to let the dogs out to have their nightly run before bedtime. I was going back into the garage when I was stopped in my tracks. I heard the scream again. But this time it sounded closer. I stepped back out into the yard about the same time the two dogs went nuts! They were barking like they were ready to attack! I called them to me, but neither dog came. I was shocked at their behavior. Both dogs were very well trained and mannered. What had gotten into them two lately? The light had a good portion of the yard lit up, and I could see them in the far right corner barking toward the mountain, the same direction the scream had come from. I walked closer and called them again. This time they came when I called, but they ran right past me! Both of them ran into the open door and the garage. Once again, their behavior shocked me. I turned around and followed the dogs into the house.

Jen and I sat out on the deck for a little while, hoping to hear the scream again. I think the dogs may have scared whatever it was, or it had heard me calling to them. Either way, there were no more screams that night. So we relaxed listening to the frogs and crickets with the occasional night birds calling.

" I can't believe how peaceful it is here," I told Jen.

"I know," she replied. "I keep expecting to hear a neighbor's stereo or TV come on at any second." She said with a laugh.

Bella barked once at the garage door, signaling us that she wanted to go out. I started to get up, "I'll get them this time," Jen said, getting to her feet.

I sank back into my chair as Jen took the dogs outside.

I watched as both dogs raced across the yard triggering the lights to come on. Jen walked down toward the river giving the dogs time to do their business. Jen was walking the length of the fence as the dogs sniffed around. All of a sudden, a raw shot of adrenaline was shot straight through my body when Jen let out a blood-curdling scream! I was instantly on my feet. For a split second, I considered jumping over the rail, then I remembered how high up it was and decided not to risk a broken neck or back.

I ran through the house and out into the back yard. Jen was now walking toward me and laughing! I stopped running and waited for her to walk to me. Both dogs alerted, then came running to me, happy to see dad outside too. My heart was still pounding in my chest, and I was struggling to catch my breath! Her scream had scared the daylights out of me!

"I am so sorry," Jen said, still laughing.
"I was watching a raccoon, and he didn't see me. He jumped on the fence toward me, and it scared me to death"! She said.

"Well, you sure got my blood pumping," I told her.
I slipped my arm around her waist as we all walked back to the house. I was ready for bed now. The sudden surge of adrenaline had left me feeling exhausted.

I stood on the back deck, watching the sunrise over the mountain. I knew I would never tire of seeing this beautiful scene every morning. I still couldn't believe how lucky we were to have found this place. I thought about the screams as I drained the last of the coffee from my cup. What could be making those cries? I had spent a lot of time in the woods and in the mountains, yet I had never heard this before. I couldn't help but be both curious and fascinated. I thought I might have to hike over in that direction one day just to see what I could find. But it wouldn't be today. Today I was going fishing, and I planned to spend the whole day on the river.

Jen had gone into town earlier to get some groceries and check the post office. I told her I would be on the river somewhere when she got back. If she needed me, she was to use our new handheld radios. I had shown her how to turn it on and radio me if needed. I placed hers on the kitchen counter and mine in my backpack.

I gathered my gear, put my waders on, and headed down to the river. Bella and Brutus were not at all happy with my leaving them in the fence. I just wasn't comfortable with them running free until I knew what kind of animal was out there, and I sure wasn't fighting with leashes while trying to fish.

I was lost in my own little world as I worked my way upstream. The fish were biting good, and I was being lulled into relaxation by the sound of the moving water. This was heaven to me. After a while, I had started to get hungry, so I walked upstream a little further, looking for a good spot to sit down. I had put some crackers and an apple in my backpack this morning. My growling stomach told me it was time to get them out.

I sat on a big rock, enjoying my snack. I didn't know how far upriver I had come, but I felt like the only person on the planet right now. There was nothing but me and the sound of the river. I was totally confused when a rock came out of nowhere and hit me right in the middle of my back!

I leaped to my feet, expecting to see some young boys running away, but there was no one there, and the forest was silent. I stood there for a moment looking for movement in the underbrush; there was nothing. Wondering how this could have happened, I sat back down on my rock. A few minutes later, a second stone whizzed past me, landing in the water. I knew now that someone was messing around. I stood up and reach inside my waders to unsnap my holster. Taking my pistol out of the holster, I started toward the underbrush on the bank. This time I was going to find out who it was. As I neared the thick brush, I heard the low growl I had heard before. It stopped me in my tracks for a moment. Whatever had growled at me before sounded like it was just on the other side of this underbrush. The brush began to move, and something big growled a little louder. I raised my gun to fire, Ready for a bear to come out in the open. But a scream came that was ear-splitting! I could feel it vibrate in my chest! This thing meant business! I turned back to the river and crossed it as quickly as I could. The only thing on my mind was getting as far away from this animal as possible! I was surprised that I hadn't broken my neck, getting across those rocks as fast as I did.

I hurriedly followed a game trail back down the side of the river. When I thought I had gone far enough, I stopped to catch my breath. I was leaning against a pine tree and trying to slow my breathing when I noticed movement on the other side of the river.

I held my breath while watching the underbrush shift from side to side. Was this thing following me? I told myself to stop thinking that way. I was only scaring myself. Then as I heard the growl, I knew there was more to it than my mind playing tricks on me. I started back down the game trail at a brisk walk. Knowing now that some animal was flanking me and running was the last thing I needed to do. I occasionally glanced to my right but never saw any signs of a bear. I can't describe how relieved I was when I made it back to our back yard. But I didn't slow down even then. I marched up the side of the fence and into the garage. In case Jen was home and watching me, I kept my steady pace right on into the bathroom. I needed a few minutes to sort out what had happened today. I was confused, scared, intrigued, and curious all at the same time. Something was out there. It might be something as simple as a rogue bear. But I was sure there was some animal out there, and it was out for blood.

It was late afternoon when I got back from my fishing trip. I took the fish out to clean them so I could get them in the freezer.

Jen drove up as I was finishing the fish. I helped her carry the bags into the house, and we started dinner together. She was tired of being in town all day, and I was a little tired myself, so we made a simple dinner and ate it in the kitchen.

Chapter 5

Jen hesitated for a moment, then said, "When I was out shopping today, I met a lady that knew about our cabin. She told me that her husband used to lease this property from the previous owners for hunting".

" I hope he's not going to ask to rent it now," I said. " I plan on using this myself."

"He won't be asking you," Jen replied. "He won't come out here anymore."

"What do you mean by that"? I asked. I knew what she was about to tell me was going to be somehow tied into this scream we had been hearing.

Well, this lady her name is Pam Kelly, said that her husband and three other men saw a Bigfoot here on the property. Well, actually, they saw a few of them.

"What"? I asked. I was shocked at what she said; I had never even thought about a Bigfoot. Weren't these things on the other side of the united states, if they even existed at all? I wasn't sure how I felt about this. The growls and screams came to mind. But I don't think I was ready to think outside the box just yet.

" Well, do you believe her"? I asked. I was wondering if Jen was thinking the same way I was.

" I really didn't know what to think." So, while I was at the library uploading my columns, I decided to do some research." I found some interesting stuff on Bigfoot." And some people that live in this area claim that they are here year round," she added. " I wanted to look up some of the sounds they made to see if it matched our scream, but I couldn't do that without speakers, and the library doesn't have them on their computers. I did the next best thing". She said with a smile." I purchased us internet service. It should be hooked up tomorrow."

I couldn't help but laugh out loud. When Jen was on a mission, nothing could stop her. If there was a Bigfoot within a thousand miles of this cabin, Jen was going to find it. Just as I thought this, a loud scream cut through the silence of the evening. Then to my amazement, it was soon answered by a deep yell higher up the mountain.

"Do you think there could be Bigfoot out there"? Jen asked, looking toward the mountain.

" I don't know," I told her. "I guess anything is possible."

"I have some pretty exciting things to show you online tomorrow," she said, reaching for my hand. "Reading some of that today sure has made me start thinking differently."

I didn't tell Jen what had happened to me earlier in the day because I didn't want to scare her. She already worried about me going out alone. I knew if I told her this, she would pace the floor the next time I left to do any hunting or fishing.

The next morning it was raining, so I was going to have to find something to do around the house. Jen was going to love this. Now she would have me doing all the small things in the house that I had been putting off.

I went to the kitchen to make coffee. Brutus was scratching at the garage door. "I'll let you out," I told him. "But I don't think you're going to like it very much." I walked through the washroom and opened the outside door. Brutus backed away from the door and the torrential rains. "Oh no, you don't," I said, pushing him on out the door. I refuse to clean up after you later". As I pushed Brutus out the door, I saw our trash cans. The lids were off of both of them, and there were paper plates scattered all over the ground. Great! I went back in to grab a jacket.

As I picked up the paper plates, I noticed that there was nothing else pulled out of the garbage, only the paper plates. Standing there in the rain, I examined the plates more closely. There were no signs of them being chewed. This just wasn't normal. I knew the wildlife would have eaten the plates and even consumed pieces and parts. There were food wrappers and meat packages that were still in the trashcan untouched. This didn't make any sense to me.

I finished cleaning up and secured the garbage lids. As I went to walk away, I turned back around. I pulled up on the trashcan lid. It didn't come off. The only way to get that lid off was to pull on both sides at the same time. Could a bear do this? But wouldn't a bear have chewed on the plates and at least pulled out a few other things? Maybe there was a homeless person somewhere on the mountain. I realized just how stupid this thought sounded. It was almost as silly as thinking I had a Bigfoot in my backyard.

Jen had the coffee done by the time I made it back to the kitchen. We sat down at the kitchen table and watched the rain create mini rivers across our back yard.

" I saw something strange this morning," I told her. I explained to her how the paper plates had been strewn around the garbage cans, and they weren't chewed up. To my amazement, Jen jumped up from the table, knocking her chair over, and raced through the garage door!
 I got up and followed. The door to the washroom was standing open, so I assumed she went out to look at the trash cans. By the time I made it to the outside door, Jen was already soaked to the skin. Her pajamas were clinging to her like wet rags, and her long hair was dripping wet. She was looking for something on the ground.

"Here it is"! She yelled triumphantly while pointing to the ground."Come here!" she yelled at me excitedly. "You have got to see this"!

I really didn't want to go out in that cold rain again, but she was excited to show me something. I took a deep breath and stepped outside. The rain felt like ice pellets on my skin. Instantly soaking my thin T-shirt. I walked over to where Jen was pointing.

"You have stepped in the middle of it," she said. "But you can still see it."

I looked down to see what appeared to be a rain-soaked footprint underneath the one I had created while cleaning up the plates.

Jen knelt down and pointed out the five toes and the heel of a bare footprint. This footprint had sunk into the rain-soaked ground.
Causing a much deeper imprint than my own shoe had caused, letting me know this had been created by something massive.
But it was the size of this print that took my breath away. It had to be at least fifteen inches long and seven inches wide!

"Holy Cow"! Was all I could manage to say.

Jen looked up at me and smiled with the rain running down her face. " I think we had a visitor last night."

" I think so too," I said, pulling her into the garage with me. We were both looking like drowned rats.

" I think we have a Bigfoot," Jen said with a big smile.

I could not believe that she was smiling about this. My Jen that was afraid she would be eaten by the wildlife was laughing at the possibility of an enormous ape-like creature running around our yard.

" And this is a good thing"? I asked her.

"Why not"? She asked. "We could actually be the first people to see them up close. We could be the first people to learn about them!" She said with excitement. "And I can't wait to show you everything I found online," she added.

Her excitement was becoming contagious. And what she said did make some sense. We could be the first people to end up getting close to them. It was eventually going to be someone, Why not us?

" Let's go get dried off," I said. "I have something to tell you."

Later in dry clothes with a hot cup of coffee, I told her what I had experienced while fishing.

"That had to of been a Bigfoot, "she said excitedly. " I think they are as curious about us as we are them," she stated.

After talking a while longer, Jen went to see if our internet had been turned on yet. It was, and we spent the rest of the day learning about Bigfoot. There were literally thousands of articles to read and videos to watch. Jen actually found Bigfoot groups on her Facebook account. All one had to do was search "Bigfoot" to see that it had taken the internet by storm. The more we read, the more the things that were happening around here made sense. I was starting to go along with Jen and believe that we actually had some Bigfoot here. It would explain a lot of the strange happenings. But I also knew that I would have to see one to fully believe that they were here.

My stomach began to growl causing me to realize that the rain had stopped and the sun was starting to set. We had spent all day learning about Bigfoot. It had only seemed like a few hours!

Jen went to start dinner while I took the dogs outside.

Chapter 6

Jen and I decided to plan a fishing trip. We would each carry cameras and audio as well as our fishing gear. In the past week, we had learned a lot, and we felt like we were ready to go out looking for signs of Bigfoot.

Jen made us some sandwiches and dropped a selection of snacks into one backpack. We would only carry one with food in it, just in case we came across a bear. She also dropped a few granola bars and some thin rope into this bag. We were going to try what some people online had suggested we do. I would be climbing a tree and tieing these granola bars well off the ground. We would give it a day or two and go back to see if anything had taken our food. I have to admit, I was anxious to see what would happen.

With the dogs outside in the fence, Jen and I were ready to go exploring.

I led the way up the game trail. Jen had asked me to take her to the place where the rocks had been thrown. She thought that might be a good area for us to begin to look around for some prints. Being that I didn't really have a plan, it sounded good to me.

By the time we made it to the place I had been, Jen was tired. She sat down on the big rock while I went to look around. I didn't really see anything. But the underbrush and leaves were pretty thick here. There was no way to find prints.

We found what we thought to be a partial print at the edge of the water. It was just to washed away for us to say for sure. Jen took a couple of pictures of it anyway. We ate our snack and began the long walk home.

We stopped a few times for me to hang up some Granola. I didn't really think this was going to work too well. I assumed the Squirrels would get to it quicker than anything. But Jen wanted to try it, so we did.

As we got back to the house, I watched as Jen opened both trashcans laying a granola bar inside on the top of each, before securing the lids back onto the cans.

" If anything gets into that tonight, you get to clean up in the morning," I told her jokingly.

" I take full responsibility." she said with a smile.

After dinner, we both took our seats out on the back deck. Right away we noticed how quiet the evening was. I felt sure we would hear something. Just as the sun began to set and long shadows were cast across the mountain we heard our first scream of the evening. Jen noted the time as being seven thirty-five. This scream was answered by a deep throaty yell.

Tonight, we didn't talk. We just sat there listening, and taking in every sound. It wasn't long before we heard our first whoop. It came from the direction we had been earlier that day. I realized then that I had actually heard this sound before. I had heard it here a couple of times. But I had heard it somewhere before. At the time I had just assumed it was some sort of bird. Where had I heard this sound? After a while, I finally remembered.

I was around fourteen or fifteen years old. My dad and I had gone hunting with my grandpa and uncle John. I had heard this whoop while I was sitting in the deer stand! I remembered it now! My heart skipped a beat when I realized that every time I heard the whoops my dad and grandpa were always ready to leave! Did they know something about Bigfoot?! They had to have known something. My father and grandfather had passed away, but my Uncle John was still alive, and just a phone call away. I debated on calling him. Would it upset him? Would he even remember? What if he didn't know anything?

A deep, throaty yell came from about fifty yards away scaring Jen and I both! We were both on our feet and in the backdoor instantly. That was just too loud and too close.

"And we are actually going to go look for this thing"? Jen said laughing.

I had to agree with her that we didn't seem very brave at the moment. I told her that we are supposed to be looking for it, and not the other way around.

We watched Bigfoot videos online until we were both too tired to keep our eyes open. That night I dreamed of multiple Bigfoot chasing Jen and me through the woods.

The next morning, Jen was a little disappointed that her trashcans were still intact. But I told her you couldn't expect to have activity every night. We decided to leave them where they were for another night or two and see what, if anything, happened.

I was going into town today to check the post office, and I thought I would swing by the hardware store to see if Tom knew anything about Bigfoot being in this area. I figured if anyone knew, it would be Tom and Nancy. Yeah, I would feel a little stupid asking, but I needed to know.

I picked up our mail and drove to the hardware store. Tom was just unlocking the door when I got there.

"Good Morning Matt," He said with a warm smile, "Come on in."

I shook Toms hand as we entered the store. Tom went into the back to make coffee, and I looked around while he was gone. I hadn't noticed before, but he had an excellent supply of camping equipment.

"Now, what can I help you with"? Tom asked, coming back around the counter. " Going to do a little camping"? he asked.

"Well, not actually," I told him. "Not yet anyway," I added.
I took a deep breath and started. Being thankful that there was no one else in the store.

"There's something I want to talk to you about," I told him.

"Wow Matt," "You look pretty serious," he said.

" I would really like to keep this just between the two of us," I stated.

Tom walked a little closer to me. "Of course Matt." That's no problem." What's on your mind friend"?

I took another deep breath. I may as well just say it, I thought. "I know this is going to sound crazy," I told him. "But, have you ever heard anything about Bigfoot being in this area"?

Tom gave me a big smile. "Of course I have!" He said. "I guess everyone in these mountains has some sort of Bigfoot story to tell."
I didn't know if I should feel anxious or relieved.

" Has someone been telling you stories"? Tom asked. "You have to watch the old timers around these parts," he added. "Sometimes they can weave a good tale."

"You are the only person I have talked to," I told him. "And the reason I am asking, Is because Jen and I have been hearing some strange screams and yells coming from the mountain."

Toms facial expression changed and became a little more serious. "Well then", He said. "Telling stories is one thing, but hearing them is something else entirely."

"What do you mean"? I asked.

"It's like I said earlier, most people around here have a story to tell. But I think only a handful have actually seen one. And that handful of individuals are the only ones that mention the screams and the yells".

"Have you ever seen one"? I asked him.

"Hell no"! He said. " I don't think I want to see one of those big beasts either." I don't get to leave the store often anyway, so my having a run in with one is pretty slim."

" I actually think Jen and I may hike up the mountain and have a look around," I said.

"Really"? Tom asked. He paused to think for a moment, then he added, "Nancy and I may tag along sometime if you don't mind."

"Hey, That would be great!" I exclaimed.

Tom and I talked a while longer. We planned to try a day hike first. Then possibly camping a night or two. The nights were still chilly, so we planned to go a few weeks from now. Tom was going to get us all set up with the backpacking equipment we would need. And I was going to get us some trail cams and audio.

I filled Tom in on everything we had experienced up at the cabin and on the river. He seemed to be as fascinated as Jen, and I was. It felt good to be able to discuss things with him and not have him think I was crazy.

We decided that Jen and I would keep records of everything going on and the time it was happening. If we could pinpoint a time these yells and screams were going on. That would give us an idea of what time we needed to be up on the mountain.

I shook Toms' hand and headed home, with a promise of keeping him updated.

Chapter 7

Jen was every bit as excited as I was to find out that Tom and Nancy would be joining us. It just felt better knowing we wouldn't be by ourselves.

I went out to the garage to grab my fishing gear. Jen had some work to get done, and I planned to get some fishing in.

As I started walking along the fence line down to the river, I was followed closely by two big mutts with very sad eyes. They hated me leaving them in the yard. I stopped and thought about it for a moment, then turned and started back for the garage. It seemed like they read my mind as they were now jumping around like playful puppies.

I slipped their shock collars over their heads and dropped the remote into my pocket. At least this would still give me a little control over them while still keeping my hands free.

I grabbed up my gear, and the three of us headed down the back yard. Brutus and Bella ran ahead of me enjoying their freedom. Brutus ran through the river and started up the trail on the other side. I reached into my pocket and gave his collar a little jolt. He turned around and came right back to me. I was well pleased that I would be able to fish now without worrying about either of them wandering off.

I cast my line out and made myself comfortable. Bella came over and sat beside me anticipating the fish I would be pulling out soon.

I couldn't understand why the fish weren't biting, then I remembered the torrential rains we had. Fishing today was probably not going to do me any good. I had tried for a little longer before I took my dogs and my gear up to the garage. I debated measuring the garage for the cabinets and shelves I wanted to put in or taking the dogs for a walk. Walking the dogs won. It didn't take me long to have them switched from shock collars to harnesses and leashes.

We went down across the yard and crossed the river. Well, the dogs crossed the river. I gave up trying to keep my feet dry and just walked through the river. We headed up the game trail on the far side. I was out to walk the dogs, so I didn't mind stopping to let them sniff around or stopping to let Brutus mark every rock and blade of grass we passed.

I didn't remember the Granola bars until Bella sniffed out the package on the trail. I reached down and picked up the empty wrapper. It didn't have any chew marks on it and looked like Jen, or I could have opened it. I assumed one of us dropped this one by accident. I crumpled it up and shoved it down in my pocket.

It was a beautiful day, and I was enjoying having the dogs out with me. I walked close by the river allowing them to run in and out of the water. They both were having a ball.

Suddenly, both of them stopped and alerted. Noses Sniffing the air and tails erect. I too stopped to see if I could hear anything. After a minute or two, the dogs relaxed, and we walked on. We came across a Granola package that was sill hanging in the tree. I jumped up to grab it. The food was gone, and I looked the wrapped over closely. This one had been chewed open at the top. It seemed like a small animal had enjoyed a treat. I stuck this wrapper down in my pocket too, and we walked on to the next one. The next wrapper was lying on the ground, and the string it was attached to was still tied to the limb and the whole limb was on the ground.

The dogs were sniffing around the limb with all of their hair standing up. I picked up the wrapper to examine it. This one had been opened like a human would do it. I put it down in my pocket and picked up the limb. The branch had not broke with the weight of a hungry animal. It had been twisted off. I knew right away that a human didn't do this. There was no way a man could have twisted that limb off. I stood there for a few minutes with my eyes scanning the woods up and down the river. I felt like something was watching me, but I couldn't see anything. It was time to take my dogs home. I was beginning to fear for their safety.

As I turned to walk off, a rock landed in the river. The dogs instantly went nuts! Brutus almost pulled me off my feet lunging in the direction the rock had come from. Both dogs were in full attack mode, and it was taking all my strength to hold them back! I had never seen either of them this way, and it caused a funny feeling in my stomach. No amount of commanding them was working. In between their barking and my commanding, I heard the growl. The hair on the back of my neck stood up.

Bella bolted and almost pulled my arm out of socket! Brutus dove in the direction the growl came from! Now I had two large dogs hell bent on going in opposite directions! The only thing I could do was to wrap the leash around Brutus's Neck and pull him back as I held on to Bella for dear life! After some struggling, Brutus finally gave in, and I got them started home.

By the time I got both dogs into the garage, I was exhausted. Heading into the kitchen, I swore to myself that I would never do that again. I wasn't twenty anymore, and I was feeling my age. I poured myself a cup of coffee and joined Jen on the back deck. It felt amazing to sit down and put my feet up.

I told Jen all about what happened up on the river and how the dogs had behaved. We both agreed that we would have to be very careful with where we walked them from now on. Our driveway might be a better option.
I pulled the Granola wrappers out of my pocket and handed them to her. After looking them over, she said,
"Now this explains a lot."

I asked her what she was talking about.

" Come on, she replied. "I have something to show you."

I followed her through the living room and out the front door to the porch. I looked at where she was pointing. Right on top of the steps were three bird feathers laid in a row. A blue bird, a red bird, and a crow. I was shocked!

"Where did these come from?" I asked her while kneeling down to get a better look at them.

"They were just here," she said. "I brought some plants out to the porch, and there they were."

I picked up the three feathers.

"What are you going to do with them"? Jen asked.

"Well, it would be rude not to accept a gift," I told her.

We decided to put a few things in a small basket and leave it in place of the feathers. Jen chose an apple, a Granola Bar (still in the wrapper.), a Banana and some Blueberries. We sat the basket on the top of the steps and went inside.

I sat back down on the back deck and picked up my cup of coffee. Just how did I actually get here I wondered. I have always been the most skeptical person in the world. And now, I am leaving treats for Bigfoot on my front porch. Had I lost my mind? Or had I stumbled upon something amazing? I wasn't sure anymore. I guess time would tell.

The next morning I went to the outside door to let the dogs into the fence. Both garbage cans had been rummaged through, and the paper plates were on the ground again. This time I was happy to tell Jen about it. She could enjoy examining the plates as she picked each one up. I was going in to make coffee.

I checked the basket on the front porch. I guess deep down I was like Jen and hoping something would be missing, but it hadn't been touched. Two days later, everything was gone, but the banana and it was tossed down at the bottom of the steps. I looked around and didn't find as much as a blueberry on the ground. It was all just gone. I had thought I would feel some kind of satisfaction once the things were taken, but I didn't. There was still no clues as to what took it or where it went. Jen and I continued to keep records on the things happening around the cabin. We noticed as the weather began to get warmer, the screams became more sporadic, yet the deep throaty yells were still happening almost every night.

We had been studying everything we could get our hands on about Bigfoot. And I'm sure we had logged literally hundreds of hours watching videos and documentaries. I know this still didn't make us experts on the subject. But it did make me just as smart as the next researcher. The way I saw it, there would be no experts until we could study one in captivity. I felt that Jen and I were as prepared as we could be.

Our hike was coming up next week, so I was making sure we had everything we might need for Bigfoot field research.

Chapter 8

Tom and Nancy arrived around seven that morning. Nancy came carrying the promised pound cake which was met with hugs and kisses from Jen. Nancy, who asked that we call her Nan, was just as excited as the rest of us. The two women got along like long lost friends. This had all the signs of being a great trip.

I didn't feel secure with leaving the dogs out all day, so I fastened them into the garage. They would be fine there until we got home.

Tom and I helped the girls into their backpacks. I had worried how Jen and Nan would be, carrying the weight of the packs plus walking uphill most of the day. Jen assured me that she would be okay and she would tell me before she became overly tired. The last thing we needed was for someone to collapse up on the mountain. We had planned to take it slow today and let everyone go at their own pace. There was no need to hurry.

After helping the girls, Tom and I Shouldered our own packs and picked up our rifles. We would be hiking up the mountain, and we wanted to be prepared for any predator that we might encounter.

Going across our backyard and looking up at this mountain. I realized we wouldn't make it far with just a day trip. But I was still eager to see what we could find.

Tom and I put the two girls in front of us. I didn't want to take the chance of a bear or a big cat sneaking up behind one of them. When the trail called for us to walk single file, we would always put the two girls in the middle. (Looking back now, it is almost funny at all the precautions we took when we were going after something that could easily rip us all to shreds.)

After about a two hour walk, we had reached the base of the mountain and were ready to start up. The girls wanted to take a quick break here. We each grabbed a bottle of water and sat down for ten minutes. To me, this was the longest ten minutes ever. I was eager to get up the mountain. The day was unseasonably warm with a cloudless sky. There was just enough of a cool breeze to keep the sun from being too hot. Days like this made me look forward to the coming summer. After the girls had gone to relieve themselves, we were ready to get started again.

The walk wasn't very steep, to begin with. And the forest floor was littered with pink lady's slippers and wild geraniums. The Mountain Laurel was just starting to bloom. I was looking around and thinking just how beautiful the woods were when I saw something that made my heart leap up into my throat!
 I immediately reach out and gently tugged Jens backpack. That was our signal for the group to stop and wait silently. Everyone turned to look at me, and I pointed at the first tree structure I had ever seen. We all looked around the forest to make sure there was no movement before we approached the structure.

It was a bunch of branches built up into a tee-pee type structure. There were many kinds of different trees used to create this. We noticed that the ground was packed down in about a six-foot radius all around it. I was mesmerized. Jen and Nan walked all around it taking pictures from every angle before we walked on. Seeing this had lifted everyone's spirits and there was a little more energy to our steps now. We came across two more similar structures not far from the first one. Again, the ground was packed down around them. The forest was mostly covered in leaf litter so we couldn't get any good prints. We saw what we thought were a few prints in the leaves, but there is no way to know for sure.

We were walking along with no one talking when Tom stopped dead in his tracks. He forgot to alert Nan, so I reached out and tugged Jens backpack.

"Listen"! Tom whispered excitedly.

I heard what I thought to be a hammer bang once on up the mountain. Why would someone be hammering out here and why only one hit? As I wondered this, the second bang came, and it was down closer to us. I felt the tiny hairs on the back of my neck stand up and a jolt of adrenaline surged through my body. I had just heard my first tree knock! It was surreal. I couldn't believe that I had just listened to a Bigfoot Tree Knock.

"Did you hear that"? Tom asked with a big smile on his face.

"Yes"! Jen replied excitedly. " It's almost like they are warning each other that we are here."

We continued our walk on up the mountain. We had been walking for a few hours, and the girls were starting to tire. Tom found us a good open area to sit and rest, and enjoy the lunch the girls had packed for us. I had told them to pack us a light lunch because we would have a long walk back and we didn't need to get sleepy after we ate. Of course, they didn't listen. I realized this when they started pulling out foot long sub sandwiches and potato chips. We enjoyed our lunch in the warmth of the sun with the cool breeze blowing up from the valley. The four of us chatted and joked like old friends. I was glad Tom and Nan had decided to come with us. Tom was wise beyond his years, and Nan was fun to be around. I already loved them both.

After we had eaten Tom and I looked around for a good spot to hang a trail camera while the girls packed up. We would need to start back now to make it home by dark. I knew it wouldn't be long before we were back up here. We had all been bitten by the Bigfoot bug.

When we got back to the Cabin Tom and Nan stayed well into the evening with us. After dinner, Jen brought out a bottle of wine, and we all enjoyed a glass on the back deck.

Tom said, "Matt, do you notice how quiet it is out here tonight? You don't hear anything but the river, no frogs, no crickets, just the river".

I told him I had noticed that from time to time but had never thought that much about it. I had never lived on the river before so I just assumed it was something natural.

He explained to me that most say the strange silence means there is a Bigfoot in the area. Everything else hides when there is an Apex predator roaming around.

Just as I opened my mouth to respond we heard a frighteningly deep yell come from just past the river! All four of us jumped!

"Holy Smokes"! Tom exclaimed. "I have never heard one so close"!

As we all sat in silence, you could hear rocks being thrown into the river. This was the sound Jen, and I had heard when we first moved in. This sound still puzzled me. Was it just throwing rocks into the river? Or was that a way that they fished? It seemed like the deeper I got into this Bigfoot stuff, the more unanswered questions I was finding.

Tom and I planned our next trip for the following week. This time we planned to go further up the mountain and stay overnight. This would allow us to walk in further and then set up camp before it became dark.

Around midnight, we hugged our new friend's goodbye, with excitement for our upcoming trip.

That night before bed, I sat down and read the notes Jen had made on our hike. This didn't look bad at all for our first time out. I felt secure in calling it a successful trip.

Chapter 9

The week had seemed to drag by, but it was finally Saturday morning. I stood looking out at the mountain with a cup of coffee in my hand. It was still hard to believe that in a few hours I would be climbing that mountain looking for Bigfoot. Had I lost my mind?

"How far do you think we will make it today"? Jen asked. Walking up and putting her arm around me. We both stood there looking at the mountain we intended to conquer.

" I want to make it as far as we possibly can," I told her. "Without pushing ourselves too hard."

" I agree," she said. "I feel that the higher up we get, the better evidence we're going to find."

I drained the last of my coffee as I heard Toms truck stop outside the garage.

Everyone was in high spirits as we gathered our equipment, and got ready for the day ahead. We sounded like four teenagers laughing and joking with one another.

This time, Tom had brought everyone a twelve-inch blade to wear on their hip, and we equipped both girls with small caliber handguns.

Everyone wore a whistle in case we got separated. Tom and I both carried a roll of painters tape in our pocket. We would tie off at random intervals as we walked.

In our excitement, it didn't take us near as long to reach the base of the mountain this time. I was both shocked and pleased with the distance we had covered. We came across a few more tree structures that hadn't been there the week before. We stopped to get pictures and let the girls take notes on our findings. Again, these structures were made by many different types of trees. They had to have been brought here just for constructing these structures. No one knows exactly why they do this or what it means. It's just more unanswered questions. But they are kind of cool to see.

We took a break at the same spot we had eaten lunch last week. It was a beautiful clearing surrounded by the forest on all sides. Instead of lunch this time, we all opted for a bag of trail mix and bottled water. We wouldn't eat a meal until we made camp.

As we started walking again, I noticed that the grade was getting steeper and we were all moving just a little slower. But that was all right. We still had plenty of time before we would need to make camp. We had walked for about ten minutes when we heard our first tree knock.
We all stopped and stood quietly anticipating the second hot dogs to come from another part of the mountain. But the solitary knock was all that we got.

We walked out of the woods onto a sandy clearing. Everyone one of us froze and didn't say a word. We were absolutely in awe at what we were looking at. In the middle of this clearing stood the biggest tree structure I had ever seen! It was easily twelve foot high. And it was constructed using full-size trees. These trees had been carried in from other parts of the forest, and some of them had to weigh at least four hundred pounds! Whatever creature created this had to be massive. Honestly, seeing this was a little frightening. There was no way humans created this. other, and there was just no way of getting something like that up here.

The ground was sandy here, so we were extremely careful when approaching this jaw-dropping creation. We hoped to find a good print. As luck would have it, Tom found one and Jen found a smaller one! There had been two here at the structure! Tom and I pulled out the casting supplies and went to work while the girls took a break. Instead of waiting for the material to dry and lifting our print. We decided to leave it and get it on our way down tomorrow. This would give it over night to set, hopefully, providing us with a very clear print.

After setting our casts, we shouldered our packs and walked on. The girls were getting tired and slowing down now. It was late afternoon, and we had been walking all day. They were both being real troopers, but you could see the fatigue in their faces. Neither had complained and would have kept pushing on, but there was no need to do this. And besides, Tom had a very good idea.

As we walked Tom had said, "Matt, let me run something by you." " Since our girls are worn out, why don't we go ahead and set up camp. You and I could grab a quick nap, and then spend the night sitting out and watching."

I really liked this idea, since most of what I had read said they move more at night. We found a nice flat area and set up our small camp. This consisted of two pup tents, a portable bathroom, and a fire pit. It wasn't home, but it would be fine for a night.

Once we got everything set up, we took turns going out to look for firewood. Jen and I went first, finding another structure pretty close to our camp. It made me a little nervous knowing they had been close to where we would be sleeping tonight.

Tom and I left the girls cooking wieners for hot dogs while we grabbed an hour nap. At first, I was worried that the smell of the food might bring in unwanted animals.

But Tom explained to me that most of them would keep their distance because of the fire. He told the girls to stay right by the fire and handed Nan his rifle. As it turned out, Nan was a great shot, and Tom said he wasn't worried about her in the least. This made me feel much better. I kissed Jen and crawled into our tent. I was more tired than I thought because I fell into an exhausted sleep right away.

When Jen woke me, it felt like I had just closed my eyes. I crawled out of the tent to a feast of hot dogs, chips, baked beans and glorious coffee. I believe those were the best hot dogs I had ever eaten in my life. I was starving and didn't even realize it.

As we ate our dinner, I didn't realize that it was getting to be late evening. We were all laughing at one of Toms jokes when the high pitched scream came from further up the mountain. It was a scream that would make your blood run cold. We were instantly silent waiting on the next vocalization. To our surprise, the next one came from down below us! Did we pass this one on the way up? It made me a little uncomfortable to have one on each side of us.

Tom and I helped the girls put the food away, and we burned our paper cups and plates. We packed the food up and hung it high in a tree outside of camp. We didn't take any chances with something bothering the girls while we were gone.

I took my rifle, leaving Toms with the girls. We grabbed flashlights and audio recorders and were all set for our night vigil. We walked out far enough to where the light from the fire didn't reach us, and we sat down.

The night was deathly still; there was absolutely no sound. Tom and I sat and stood for hours just listening. We would hear an occasional wood knock or a distant yell. Other than that, there was nothing. I was getting ready to tell Tom that I didn't think anything was going to happen when I heard the distant footsteps! The footsteps were walking through the leaves, so there was no mistaking what it was. The steps continued to grow closer and closer. My heart was pounding in my chest, and I was unknowingly holding my breath. You could tell by the sound that this creature was bipedal and had a large gate. These steps came right up to Tom and me and passed within six feet of us! I wanted so bad to turn my light on and see this thing, but something told me not to. I wanted to gain their trust. This was our first trip of what I hoped would be many, so there was no need in possibly scaring them away from this area. We listened as the footsteps went around our camp and faded away. They had stayed at the same pace, they never sped up or slowed down. It was like it knew exactly where it was going. After this, Tom and I called it a night and tried to get a couple of hours of sleep before sun up.

The next morning we had coffee and filled the girls in on the phantom footsteps. Jen said that she had heard it too and it scared her to death. Nan was upset that she had fallen asleep and missed it.

We put our fire out and packed up camp. While I made sure we left no coals burning, Tom went to get the food bag. He came back with news that shocked and amazed us all.

Tom said as he approached the tree we had tied the food up in he could see a large tree limb lying on the ground. He walked over to it and it was the limb the backpack was tied to. The backpack was still securely tied, but the limb had been twisted off and pulled down! He said it scared him for a moment when he saw this because he had not looked around to see if anything was watching him when he approached the tree. And he knew whatever had taken this branch down was huge.

He untied the backpack so he could examine it. The zipper had been pulled apart. And the bags of trail mix were missing. The wieners, chips, and extra hot dog buns were sill untouched. The only other thing missing was Nan's pink bandanna. And she had tied it securely to the outer strap of the pack. Something was able to untie this banana in order to take it. Once again, there were no footprints due to leaves. We moved the food to another pack and began our long walk home.
We were all exhausted by the time we made it back down to the casts we had left in the ground. They gave us all a welcomed excuse to sit down and rest for a while.

Tom and I gently dug those prints up; treating them like they were gold bars. We got out two of the prettiest sets of prints I had ever seen. We were all thrilled! Tom pulled out his tape measure. The first one was sixteen inches long and seven across. The second one was fifteen inches long and five across. I couldn't wait to get these home and get them cleaned up.

After our short break, we got started again. It was another beautiful day with just a few high clouds in an endless blue sky. We stopped by our clearing for me to grab the trail camera we had left last week. Everyone was ready for another break, so we all rested and had a can of soda.

We had heard the occasional tree knock but other than that our walk was uneventful. We made it back to the cabin about four. I thought we had made really good time.

Tom and I sat down at the table and planned our next trip. He had hired someone to run the store on the weekends now, so it would free up his time for research. This time, we were going further up. We knew this trip would take us two to three days.
 I wasn't sure the girls would be able to handle this. But Tom and I were determined. The more evidence we found, the more we wanted to find.

We were all tired so Tom and Nan didn't stay very long this time. Jen and I ate a sandwich for dinner and went through the images on the trail Camera. I was excited when I inserted the SD card into my laptop. We had every possibility of having a Bigfoot image. As it turned out, we had a black bear and a lot of deer. Raccoon and squirrels and then the trail cam was tilted down. I had to assume a squirrel must have landed on it. The rest of the images were nothing but the ground. I would purchase a second trail camera and make my odds a little better.

Chapter 10

The following week I ordered two more trail cameras and two pairs of night vision binoculars. To go along with our night vision cameras. When Jen asked me what I had paid for them, I told her to just be happy that I didn't buy the Flir I had been eyeing. I knew eventually I would have to get one, but that could wait. I had purchased a thermal a couple of years ago for hunting. But I had yet to buy the flir.

Tuesday afternoon Tom called and wanted to know if Jen and I could come down to the store. He wouldn't tell me what it was about. But Jen and I hopped into my truck and headed to town.

When we got to the store, besides Toms truck there was only one other car in the parking lot. Jen and I went in and were immediately greeted by a smiling Tom.

" I'm so glad you two could come," he said. "There is someone here I want you to talk to. A dear friend of mine came by to visit today, and I asked him if he would tell you two about his story. He has agreed to, and he is waiting in the back room where you all can talk in private". Tom motioned us to come around the counter and follow him to the back room.

Tom opened the door to a small room with a refrigerator, microwave, coffee pot and sink on one side. A large table with six chairs in the center and a couch on the far wall. An older gentleman sat at the table with a cup of coffee. His gray hair shown beneath a worn camouflage cap.

Tom said, "Matt, I would like you to meet John." I smiled, as he introduced me to my Uncle John.

After Uncle John's initial shock had worn off, he stood up, and we hugged. I would never have expected this! I was thrilled to see Uncle John looking so well. I was sure he had to be in his mid to late seventies.

Tom was thrilled when he found out that John and I were actually related. It seemed that these two had been friends for a long time. Tom went back out to wait on customers and left Uncle John and me to catch up.

Jen made us a cup of coffee and refilled Uncle Johns cup. We talked about the old days and family that we haven't seen. We remembered those that had passed and talked about the ones that were sick. The conversation began to slow, and I was ready to ask my question.

"Uncle John," I began. "What can you tell me about Bigfoot?"

"What is it that you want to know son?" He asked.

"Have you ever seen one"? I prodded.

"I sure have," Replied Uncle John. " I have seen them a few times. And those are memories that I will never forget". He said.

"Can you please tell us about it?" I asked

" Of course I can." He responded. "The details leading up to my sightings sometimes gets foggy because it was so long ago. But I will tell you as best I can remember." He said.

"I guess my first sighting is the one I remember the most. I was about thirty years old. A buddy and I had planned to go deer hunting one morning. It was cold, and we had about six inches of new snow on the ground. We had planned to deer hunt until day break and then we would look for some rabbits. When we got out to the woods, it was about four in the morning and still very dark. Bill headed out to the east, and I went west. We would meet back at the truck at sun up. I walked about a quarter of a mile in the dark. My footsteps were making crunching noises in the ice. I was trying my best to be quiet and not alert anything that I was there. But there was a thin layer of ice on the snow that made being quiet impossible. I finally found a good spot about a quarter of a mile from the truck. I knelt down beside a big evergreen tree knowing some of the big branches would obscure me.

Just as I got settled in, I heard this strange bird that I had never heard before. I know that you have heard it too Matt. " He said, looking over at me. "It went Whooooop! Shortly after, I listened to another one answer. I didn't pay too much attention to this because there are probably many birds out there that we have never heard before. I just assumed this was one. I was knelt there by my tree being as quiet as a mouse. After a while, I heard the footsteps of another hunter. He passed pretty close to my tree and went on down the bank toward a small stream. I didn't think anything about it. It was just another hunter finding his spot before daybreak.

As the sun began to come up, I became more alert.

I was hoping the deer would be moving up from the stream and pass by me. I readied my gun and waited. I heard this other hunter coming up from the creek. I became quite annoyed with him because his moving about was going to ruin my chances of getting a deer. With the sun just beginning to lighten the sky I still couldn't see very far. So I waited for him to get closer. I saw his head come up over the hill and I thought, this is a pretty big man, and I'm not about to say anything to make him mad. I thought my eyes were playing tricks on me. When this man topped the hill, he was huge. I couldn't see any detail then because he was still too far away. But even the dark shape let me know this was the biggest man I had ever seen. As he drew closer, I began to realize that this wasn't a man at all.

As it got closer to me, I saw that it was covered in dark hair. It's head had an almond shape to it with what looked like a short Mohawk going down the center. The skin on its face and hands looked like a dark leather. This thing had hands just like a human, but the arms were just a little longer than ours. I was absolutely terrified. I knew I was looking at a real monster. This thing walked right past me without stopping. I could hear my heart pounding in my ears, and I was holding my breath. I was praying it wouldn't see me kneeling there underneath the branches. After it had passed by me, I stayed there a while to scared to move. What if this thing was somewhere behind me, watching me. I finally got up enough nerve to stand up on trembling legs and make a b-line back to the truck. When my buddy showed up, he could tell something was wrong. After much prodding, I finally told him what had happened. He got all excited saying I had seen a Bigfoot. He wanted to go back and look for tracks while I just wanted to get the heck out of there.

A few weeks later I let my friend talk me into going back out there and looking for tracks. This time, I took my Elk hunting gun with me. I was not going back out there without being fully armed. My buddy laughed at me, but he had not seen what I had. This monster was no joke. We got back to the spot I had been at when I saw it. There were no tracks that we could see some snow had melted and refrozen then we had more snow off and on so I knew the tracks were probably gone by now.

We walked on down the hill and crossed the small stream. And right there just as plain as day, were a set of prints leading up the opposite hill. I don't know how big these prints were, But I wore a size thirteen boot, and I put my foot into one of those prints and my big old foot looked small. We followed these prints about a mile through the woods, and then they just stopped. I don't know how or why, but they just stopped. My buddy thought it might have climbed up into the trees, and I guess it could have. That's the only way I could explain those footprints just stopping. I went out with my friend one more time after that. I heard that strange bird, but there was no snow on the ground, so we didn't find any footprints to follow. My buddy continued to go up there on the mountain looking. But I never went back. I didn't want to see this thing again.

When Uncle John stopped to drink his coffee, I could see that he was getting tired. I wanted to hear about his other sightings, but I didn't want to push him.

'Wow," Jen said. "That had to be terrifying!"

"It was," said Uncle John. "I dreamed about it for years after."

" I can't thank you enough for talking to us Uncle John," I said.

"If it's OK with you, I would like to do this again sometime soon."

" I would like that," He said with a smile." You kids come by the house whenever you want to".

We all stood up and exchanged hugs. I thanked Tom and walked Uncle John out to his car. I was thrilled to have him in my life again. And talking to him today had been amazing.

When we got out to his car, Uncle John looked at me, and his face was serious. " Tom told me about you guys hiking on the mountain. That is some dangerous territory and a massive animal that you are messing around with. Promise me that you will be careful." he said.

I promised him that we were being very careful with what we were doing. And just as soon as I could get me a few good photos, I would be through. I didn't know in my heart if this were true or not, But I didn't want my Uncle John worrying about me.

He gave me another hug before getting into his car.

Chapter 11

I was pouring myself a cup of coffee. We would be leaving for our hike in the morning, and I needed to talk to Jen. I had been running this conversation through my mind. I just wasn't sure how it was going to go.

Jen was out on the deck sitting in the morning sun with her coffee. I took mine out and joined her at the table.

Before I could ever say anything, Jen looked me dead in the eye and said, "No matter what you say to me, I am going with you tomorrow."

"What makes you think I was going to say anything"? I asked innocently.

"Because I know you," Jen replied. "You and Tom think this trip may be too hard for Nan and me. And I have already made up my mind. If you are going, then I am going. We started this together, and I'm not about to stop now".

Jen could really be bull headed if she needed to. But that was one thing I admired about her. She wasn't a quitter.

"OK then," I said with a smile. "I will be happy to have my Bigfoot partner with me this weekend."

But deep down, I was worried that she and Nan may have a hard time keeping up in such rugged terrain. The higher we climbed, the tougher it was going to get.

The next morning dawned bright and sunny. I heard Nan before I ever knew they had arrived. Jen and I walked out to the garage. Nan was giving Tom a heck of a time. Nan looked over at Jen and said, "Do you believe this old goat thought he was going to leave me at home"? " I think I'd better check him for a fever" Nan added, coming over to give Jen and myself hugs.

Tom was bent over the side of his pickup truck zipping up a backpack. He looked up at me sheepishly and said, " I tried to leave her behind, but she chased the truck about three-quarters of a mile, and I had to slow down, I thought I would blow the engine in my old truck."

We all busted out laughing as we began to gather our gear. The trip would be longer this time, so we each had about twice as much to carry. Again, the men double packed their own bags trying to leave the girls as light as possible. The food we took this time was minimum. We had hoped to supplement with hunting and fishing.

As we loaded up our gear, Tom passed out handheld radios to everyone. He mumbled something about "better safe than sorry." I thanked him, and then pulled out the surprise I had for him. I passed him his new set of binoculars. He was absolutely thrilled. He kept trying to pay me for them, but there was no way I was going to let him, so we agreed on a handshake and a hug.

Once again, we helped the girls shoulder their packs and then helped each other. We were all carrying a little more weight this time so I knew we wouldn't be walking near as fast. But that was OK. Tom and I had planned to camp Friday night, then move higher up on Saturday, then we would stay Saturday night and start back home on Sunday.

The weather was beautiful and sunny. The weatherman had said that we may have some rain on Saturday evening, so we were prepared.

The four of us headed toward the mountain. My Uncle John's warning kept going through my head. I knew this was just because of his story that he had told us, but none the less. It kept playing over in my mind.

This time when we reached the base of the mountain we didn't stop for a break. We were going to try to push on to the first clearing. We were now calling this "The Meadow." If we could get to the meadow, it would be a good place for everyone to rest and have a snack.

There was a light breeze blowing as we walked it was early May, and the foliage on the mountain was in full bloom. The Pine trees were just starting to release their scent, and the daffodils were popping up everywhere. I was enjoying the beauty of nature while we walked. The girls seemed to be managing a little better this time. When we finally made it to the meadow, everyone was tired. We shrugged out of our backpacks and sat down on the green grass.

I was pleased to see what the girls had packed. We all had an apple, a handful of peanuts and some cheddar cheese along with a sports drink. This was exactly what we needed to keep us going. I bragged on my Jen for being so thoughtful. As we were eating, Tom said,
"Well, would you look at that."

Just at the edge of the woods was a huge X. It had been made with some heavy limbs. This X was placed exactly where we would be walking when we head on up the mountain. Uncle Johns warning flooded my mind.

Tom and I sat up a trail camera pointing to where this X had been made. I was very careful to make sure I camouflaged it so it wouldn't be seen. We skirted around the X and headed on up the mountain.

I wanted to go further than where we had camped last time. Everyone was quiet for the most part while we were walking. We didn't want to take a chance on missing a tree knock or a vocalization.

We stopped at the sandy clearing where the big tree structure was, and looked around for some prints. Not seeing anything we moved on.

It was late afternoon by the time we passed the area where we camped last time. We put a trail cam here because we had heard the footsteps. Tom and I wanted to get at least two more hours in before we stopped to set up camp.

Our walking became a little slower as the woods grew thicker. The underbrush wasn't easy to get through. I found myself digging out my hatchet and using it to get through some of the brush. As we pushed on through the woods, I began to wonder if we were going to make it out of them before dark. I knew that we could set up camp in the woods if we had to. But I preferred an open area where we could build a really nice fire. A cup of coffee would be pure heaven right about now.

We finally came out of the woods into a clearing. It wasn't big, but it would be okay for the night. We set up the tents and rounded up some firewood.

It was completely dark by the time we got the fire lit. After dinner, Tom and I decided to just sit by the fire while it died out and see if we heard anything. We would have to get us some sleep tonight to be able to cover a good distance tomorrow. While using my binoculars I had thought, I saw something in the trees, but I couldn't be sure. It looked like a tall figure had been standing there watching us and when I saw it, it stepped back behind the tree.

I dreamed about Bigfoot that night and woke up in a cold sweat.

It was still dark outside, but the sun would be coming up soon. Jen was snoring gently beside me as I crawled out of the tent.

I took my flashlight and walked to the edge of the woods. I needed to relieve myself and find some firewood to get some coffee started. I had to go further into the forest to find some wood. As I was picking up limbs, my blood went cold. Not ten feet from me, I heard 'whoop"! Somewhere just past our tents came a knock! I stood there holding my breath and not moving a muscle. I was trying to hear any movement that might tell me where they were. Not hearing anything I quickly grabbed some wood and hurried back to camp.

After breakfast that morning I told everyone what had happened. And Tom said it wouldn't hurt to keep our guard up from here on out. We were moving further into their territory now, and they may become aggressive.

I wondered how Tom knew this, and then I remembered all the stories he had heard over the years. Surely there had to be a few people that had stories about this mountain.

I was pleased that it was still early when we got started on up the mountain. This would be our last night, so I wanted to push as far as we could. I left my second trail camera here since we had some activity.

We hadn't been walking long when Tom signaled for us all to stop. In a very small voice, he said he thought he heard something flanking us to the left. None of us looked in that direction. He said he had been listening to it for a little bit and he wanted us all to be aware. Tom and I held our guns a bit more ready as we walked on.

Tom was right. I could now hear the footsteps in the leaves matching our own. I was shocked that I had not heard this earlier. I watched as Jen unsnapped her pistol. I knew that she was hearing it now too. I was focusing on the steps to our left when a tree knock came from our right. It sounded like it was kind of close.

We all continued our steady walk. I would cut my eyes to the left from time to time hoping to catch a glimpse of whatever this was. I never saw anything and eventually the footsteps stopped.

For most of the day, we were walking uphill through thick forest. It was well past lunch time before we ever stopped for a snack. This had been a really tough hike and the girls were doing good. I actually found myself getting winded a couple of times. I wanted to let everyone rest a while before we moved on.

After we had all rested, Jen was on her knees putting the remaining food back into the pack when she let out a yelp. She said she had been hit in the back, right between her shoulder blades with a rock! Looking behind her she picked up the rock she had just been hit with. As I stood up to walk over to her, I was hit in the leg with a rock! Tom and I went toward the section of woods they had seemed to be coming from, we didn't see anything but a single rock come out of the woods. We waited there for a few minutes when nothing else happened. We got into our backpacks and headed on up. Just as we started walking, we heard a single knock come from higher up the mountain. I knew they were watching us.

The further up the mountain we made it, the more tree structures we were seeing. We were flanked a couple of times by another unseen bipedal friend (or enemy). It was beginning to get frustrating to have all of this evidence that they were here, but nothing substantial that would tell others, "Look, these creatures exist."

We were stopping more often now to let everyone catch their breath. I don't know if it was the fact that we were all tired or the fact that we were at a higher elevation now but we were all getting winded quicker than we had.

One after the other, we pushed through thick forests and clearings. We took pictures of tree structures and documented everything we found. We kept audio recorders running at all times catching yells, tree knocks, and grunts. (And again, none of this could be used as solid proof.) I found myself thinking about Uncle Johns story and what I wouldn't give to have that experience. Unlike Uncle John, I was equipped to get images and video. That is all the proof I would ever need.

As we were pushing through some thick underbrush, it was nearing time for another break when a yell came from higher up the mountain that made my hair stand on end! This was deeper than I had ever heard before. To me, it sounded like a male stating his claim to his territory. It caused us all to stop dead in our tracks.

After this, Tom said it wouldn't hurt to start keeping our eyes open for a good camping spot. We didn't want to try setting up camp after dark because it would be hard to tell about our surroundings. He was right because the sun was beginning to cast long shadows through the trees.

Chapter 12

After another hour we pushed through the woods to a clearing. Jen and Nan dropped their packs to the ground and sat down. I knew then that they had gone far enough. Tom went a little further ahead to check out the area while I scoped out the surrounding woods.

When Tom came back, he walked over to where I was, gathering firewood.

" Matt, It wouldn't hurt for us to keep our guns at the ready tonight," he said. "Just over that knoll is a stream. That creek will bring in the wildlife which in turn will bring in the Squatches," he told me.

This was music to my ears! This might just prove to be the area we needed to get our solid proof. I couldn't help but give Tom a huge smile which he returned immediately. We gathered up some firewood and helped the girls set up camp.

The clouds had begun to move in taking away any chance of moonlight tonight. I just hoped the rain would hold off.

The girls outdid themselves again with Bratwurst, baked beans and a potato cooked on the coals along with some amazingly strong coffee.

I had been tossing an idea around in my head while we ate. I wanted to run it by Tom and see what he thought. I waited until It was time to go look for more firewood then I could talk to him without the girls hearing us.

I told Tom I had been thinking about pushing on up the mountain a little tonight, then we could come back to camp and bed down a few hours before we started for home in the morning.

Tom said he wasn't really crazy about moving in the dark, but if that's what I felt like we should do, he was more than willing.

We took the firewood back to camp, and I told the girls what I was thinking about. Nan was totally against it, but Jen agreed that might be our best chance to get the proof we wanted. That is why we had even come up here in the first place.

We all grabbed an hour nap. Tom hung a lantern high in a tree so we would be able to find our camp. We put out the fire, grabbed our weapons, a small amount of equipment, and started toward the knoll.

With me leading, we all walked single file. I was moving slow and trying to make sure the path I was creating was good enough for everyone to follow. We didn't need to lose anyone on this mountain in the dark.

We would walk so far and then stop and turn our lights out. We would stand in this one area for about thirty minutes just listening. We were beginning to get a light mist, and it was becoming foggy. Nan asked how in the world we expected to see anything in this. Tom explained to her that if they were hidden by the fog, then we were too, and this would be the best opportunity to see one.

We had stopped walking and was listening. I was looking through the Thermal but not picking up anything when Jen moved closer to me. Putting her mouth near my ear, she whispered, "I'm getting scared." I immediately pulled her close to me and told her we would be going back to camp soon. I still wanted to go a little further, but I would keep her close to me, and she'd be okay.

I'm not sure how far from camp we had gotten, I wasn't even concerned with that. We had stopped again and was listening. The only sound was an occasional drop of rain from a limb. I was looking through the thermal, when I saw something to our right, it was huge and moving very fast through the woods going up the mountain. It was almost too fast for me to realize what I was seeing! I sucked in my breath causing the others to immediately pan to the right, but it was already gone. I told the others in a loud whisper that I had just seen a Bigfoot!

A branch behind us popped very loudly! We all spun around just in time for Nan to be hit by a rock! About the time Nan let out a yelp, we heard a branch snap loudly behind us again! This was the direction we had come up. It seemed as if we were being pushed on up the mountain! After the branch had snapped, it was followed by a deep guttural growl! Were they surrounding us?

(Why was I not catching anything on thermal? I wasn't getting any heat signatures at all!) Nan and Jen were snapping pictures rapid fire with their night vision cameras. This growl was menacing and made my hair stand on end. It was coming at us from every direction! My heart was pounding! And a cold sweat beaded up on my forehead. I was suddenly filled with a sense of dread. I released my thermal to hang around my neck and readied my gun. The sudden growl had caused us all to move a few steps forward on up the mountain. Just as we shifted forward, something not far from us let out a yell that I swear vibrated through the whole mountain! It was a deep and long yell that jarred through my chest like a base drum!I think I even felt the vibration in my feet! Just then came a thunder of branches being broken and whole trees being pushed over as if someone had released twenty bulls up on this mountain and they were all heading for us! In a split second, we all turned to run! This thing was coming fast! We were trying to run back down this mountain, but the fog kept us from seeing good, and the rain had everything slick.

We were all slipping and tumbling down this mountain as something gigantic chased us! Thank God Tom had the sense of mind to get us turned toward the woods. We could use the trees to hold ourselves up. We were running through the trees as Branches and trees broke behind us! The sound of those trees crashing was as loud as a bulldozer! It was absolutely horrifying!

Tom just kept yelling, "Go!","Go!","Go!",

I was no longer trying to choose an easy path. I had lost all sense of direction. Now it was a game of survival! I just ran. Trying to put as much distance between us and this thing as possible! As long as we were heading down, we had to be going in the right direction. My feet kept sliding out from under me on the wet leaves. I would fall down and scramble to get back on my feet to keep running! Finally, I realized that the noise behind us had died down. I began to slow down and came to a stop. Just as I turned around, a sobbing Jen ran into my arms, as Nan stood there trying to catch her breath with a haunted look on her face.

"Where is Tom"? I screamed at her. I didn't mean to shout at her, I believe the fear and adrenalin just caused it to come out as a scream. I immediately felt horrible about it when I saw her expression turn to pain as she looked behind for Tom.
"He was right behind me", she mumbled. "TOM"! , "TOM"!
"TOOOOOOM"! She screamed. As her screams began to die down, we heard branches breaking above us. I was praying it was Tom until I heard the growl.

"RUN"! I screamed at the girls. I pushed them both down the mountain in front of me, and we were all running again with Jen in front this time.

I'm not sure how far we ran, It seemed like we ran forever. The rain had gotten harder and the night was getting colder. When we finally stopped again, my side was killing me with a sharp knife like pain and I felt like I couldn't run another step. All three of us were trying to control our breathing as we gasped for air.

"What direction do we go now," Jen asked, still gasping for air. I looked around at our surroundings and realized that I had no clue where we were. And I know longer had my rifle in my hands! Where was my damn gun?!

"Matt"! Jen said, "Which way is camp"?

" I don't know," I told her in a small voice. It killed me inside to admit this to her, I knew how scared she was.

"What do you mean,"" You don't know""? She asked me.
"Where is our camp"?

"We got all turned around while we were running," I told her.

"That is where Tom is"! Nan blurted out, sounding excited. " I'm sure he is back at camp waiting for us"! I hoped with everything in me that she was right.

The rain had begun to come down hard. We were all soaked to the skin, and I had no clue where we were. We were all shivering from the cold, and the possibility of hypothermia was very real. I knew I would never be able to make a fire in this heavy rain. All I could do was to keep us all moving for warmth. And with any luck, we would find our camp.

"Let's go find our camp," I told the girls.

We were all looking for the lantern that Tom had hung in the tree. This time when we started walking, I realized that my boots were feeling really tight. This was a sure sign that my feet were swollen. All I could do about it was keep walking. I was hoping that they would eventually go numb from the cold and wet then the pain wouldn't be so bad.

With every step, I knew that running into a Bigfoot was a possibility. It caused my stomach to stay in knots and my heart to beat faster than it should. If I was feeling this way I could only imagine the terror the girls must be feeling.

I had never been a real spiritual guy. But I began to pray as I walked. Our situation was pretty dire, and if prayer could help, then I was all for praying.

I don't know how far or how long we walked. But I know I literally could not put one foot in front of the other. I stopped and leaned on a tree, trying to catch my breath. Jen and Nan sat down on the wet ground. I wanted to be off my feet so bad that I just slid down the tree beside them.

The rain was still coming down, and it sounded loud hitting the leaves. Jen began to cry gently beside me, and Nan soon joined her. I reach up to wipe the water off my face, and I saw the blur of light ahead! I thought I was seeing things. I wiped my eyes and looked again! It was a light, but it wasn't our camp, this light was moving. I strained my eyes to try to make out what this was. Then it hit me, It had to be Tom! Tom was looking for us!

"Tom"? I called. Trying to be loud enough that he could hear me but not loud enough to alert anything else. The light made a wide circle letting me know he heard me! The girls instantly looked up as I called out to Tom.

Nan jumped to her feet and took off running! "Nan don't!" I yelled.

But she was running toward the light yelling "Tom"! "Tom"! "Here we are"!

Jen and I both were on our feet now as we watched Nan approach the light.

Hearing Toms laughter was music to my ears!! Jen and I hurried behind Nan.

The four of us were all laughing and hugging in the pouring rain.

We followed Tom back to camp just as the sun started to come up. One of our tents had been torn up pretty badly, and the backpacks had been rummaged through. Our stuff was strewn everywhere. None of us cared. We all crawled into the one tent and slept.

It was almost noon when we got up. We found what was left of our food and Jen made us some coffee. We ate and then salvaged as much of our gear as we could. We loaded up and headed down the mountain. We just wanted to get home.

It was almost three in the morning when we walked into our back yard. Tom and Nan stayed in our guest room.

We all suffered some damage to our feet. Jen fixed us all tubs of hot water and Epsom salts as we had coffee. We looked like a bunch of crazy old people, all sitting on the deck soaking our feet. But it sure felt like heaven.

None of us have been back up on the mountain since this happened. I keep telling myself that I need to go back and get the trail cameras and look for my gun. But so far, I haven't been in any hurry.

We all would like to go back sometime and try to make it to the top of the mountain. Who knows, maybe one day we will.

If you enjoyed this book, please consider leaving a review.

Also, you might want to check out some of Melissa's other titles.

1. **<u>Bigfoot Chronicles,</u> A true story**

2. **<u>Bigfoot Chronicles 2,</u> A true story**

3. **<u>Sasquatch, The Native Truth</u>. A true story**

4. **<u>Sasquatch, The Native Truth. Kecleh-Kudleh Mountain</u> A true story**

5. **<u>Sasquatch, The Native Truth. Ravens Return</u> A true story**

6. **<u>The True Haunting of a Paranormal Investigator</u>**

7. **<u>Dog Man</u>, A True Encounter**

8. **<u>Black-Eyed Kids. My Three Months of Hell</u>. A true story**

9. **<u>Family Ties</u>. Fiction**

10. **Female Bigfoot Encounters**. True Stories

11. **Our Paranormal Reality, A True Haunting. Book 1 The Early Years**

12. **Our Paranormal Reality, A True Haunting. Book 2 The Investigation**

13. **Bigfoot, A New Reality. A True Story**

14. **The Birth of a Psychic with Telekinesis. A True Story**

15. **Lifting the Veil on All Things Paranormal, True Stories**

16. **Desolate Mountain, One woman's true story of survival**.

17. **The Watcher, A true story**.

18. **Bigfoot Found me. One man's true encounter with Bigfoot**.

19. **Goodbye. A true story of an Ouija board experience**

20. <u>**Sasquatch Travels. Based on a true story**</u>

21 <u>**Dream House**</u>

22. <u>**Breast Cancer, Faith, God & Home Free**</u>

23. <u>**Wood Bugger. One boy's true story of growing up with Bigfoot**</u>

24. <u>**The Doll**</u>.

25. **A Week in Bigfoot Territory**

Melissa's books can be found online at

Amazon

Barnes and Noble

Books a Million

Wal-Mart

and your local

bookstore.

Follow Melissa on,

Her Blog;

http://www.melissageorge.net/

Facebook;

https://www.facebook.com/MelissaGeorgeParanormalAuthor/

Twitter;

https://twitter.com/AuthorMelissaG

Pinterest;

https://www.pinterest.com/melissa6144/

Instagram;

https://www.instagram.com/authormelissageorge/

Get sneak peeks on upcoming books. And enjoy book giveaways with every new release!

http://melissageorge.net/

About the Author.

Melissa was born and raised in a small town in upstate South Carolina. She first became a well-known Blogger and later decided to take her writing a step further. Her first book, My Paranormal Life, A True Haunting, started out as her own private journal of her family dealing with a dark entity. But it doesn't stop there, Melissa took it even further and let her experiences help her to co-found a paranormal team and a cryptid team. She enjoys being able to reach out and help others. She has made many new friends in both of these fields, which has also led her to help others to have their story told. Melissa realizes first hand that these people have a very passionate and unique story that needs to be told. In getting these compelling stories out to the public, she hopes it will help further research in both of these fields, and just maybe the individual that shares their story with her may find some closure to their own personal nightmare. Melissa feels honored to be able to bring you true stories of the unexplained.

If you have a story you would like to see published or just want someone to talk to. I promise you complete anonymity.
Melissageorge143@gmail.com

Manufactured by Amazon.ca
Acheson, AB

12740361R00059